The Compelling Community Study Guide

Mark Dever and Jamie Dunlop

:: CROSSWAY®

WHEATON, ILLINOIS

The Compelling Community
Study Guide

Contents

How to Use This Study Guide

The Compelling Community (Crossway, 2015) was written to help churches recapture a biblical vision for church community in all of its life-giving glory. As such, it was written primarily with church leaders in mind. However, in the years since it was published, many other Christians have found it to be quite profitable, and many small groups have used it as well.

Whether you're reading this by yourself, in a group of two or three, or in a larger group, this study guide is designed to help you apply the principles presented in *The Compelling Community*. Most importantly, it is designed specifically for those who may not currently serve in church leadership.

Suggested Schedule

The main ideas in *The Compelling Community* are concentrated near the beginning of the book. Part 1 is the meat of the book, and the remaining chapters help put those big ideas into practice. As a result, I encourage you to focus your discussion and reflection time on the first four chapters. The questions in the study guide are written with that pace in mind. Here's a suggested schedule:

- Meeting 1: Chapter 1 (Two Visions of Community)
- Meeting 2: Chapter 2 (A Community Given by God)
- Meeting 3: Chapter 3 (Community Runs Deep)
- Meeting 4: Chapter 4 (Community Goes Broad)
- Meeting 5: Chapters 5–6 (Preach and Pray)
- Meeting 6: Chapters 7–8 (Relationally Oriented Ministry)
- Meeting 7: Chapters 9–10 (Discontentment and Sin)
- Meeting 8: Chapters 11–12 and the Conclusion (Evangelism and Church Planting)

If you're feeling pressed for time, your group might consider studying only the first four chapters, leaving people to peruse the last eight by themselves. On the other hand, groups with more time have found it useful to discuss chapter 4 across two meetings. In that case you might want to look at Ephesians 2:11–3:21 and discussion questions 1–3 in the first meeting and the remaining questions in the second meeting.

Passages for Study

This guide lists a passage of scripture to be studied with each chapter of the book. Some of these passages are addressed at length in the book and some are not. Most are addressed in the study guide. In a group setting, you might encourage each person to think through the passage before the group meets and then share reflections on that passage before you discuss the assigned book chapters. Generally, the first question or two in each section pertains to the suggested passage for study.

Some of the passages are quite short, and I intend for you to think about each verse carefully. Some passages are more lengthy. For these lengthier passages, my intent for the purposes of this study guide is for you to focus on the overall message and texture of the passage rather than studying all of it in-depth.

A Note about How to Use This Book to Serve Your Church

Reading a book like this, especially if you're not a church leader, has the potential to equip you to serve your church better, but it also risks equipping you as a discouraging critic of your church. In that sense, it carries some of the same risks and opportunities of a teenager reading a book about marriage and then thinking about his parents' marriage. After all, you are not the one making most of the day-to-day decisions in your church, and this book may sometimes make you question the wisdom of those making the decisions. Imagine how your pastor will feel if, having read the book, you come to him full of ideas for how he needs to do his job better. That would be unfortunate.

As such, the questions in this study guide generally avoid asking you to assess or criticize your church. Instead, where assessment and criticism seem warranted, they focus on assessing and criticizing *you* and *your view* of your church. With that in view, please keep a few priorities in mind as you read:

1. Praise and thanks. Rather than using this book to articulate where your church leaders can do a better job, use it to praise God for what *he* has done to build biblical community in your church. I hope that your main response as you read is not criticism but thanksgiving.

2. Trust. If your church doesn't do some things you see in this book, don't assume your church leaders haven't thought of them or are opposed to them. There may well be good reasons to do things differently than what I suggest. Or it

may be that your pastor *does* like these things, but he's being patient, waiting for the right time to put them into place.

3. Encourage. By all means, talk with your pastor or other church leaders about what you're learning from this book, but do so with the primary goal of *encouragement*, not criticism. Heaven knows that church leaders can always use more encouragement! Assume that they see the same things in the Scriptures that you see about the church, and talk with them about how you can help your church grow to be more biblical.

4. Pray. Turn the insights of this book into prayers for your congregation. I hope that you consider a more informed prayer life to be an excellent outcome from reading this book. Prayer is in no way restricted to church leaders, and it is powerful.

Special thanks to Edgewater Baptist Church in Nashville, Tennessee, and the International Evangelical Church in Duhok, Iraq, for piloting this study guide before it was published.

With prayer for you as you read and discuss this book,

Jamie Dunlop
Associate Pastor
Capitol Hill Baptist Church

PART 1

A VISION FOR COMMUNITY

1

Two Visions of Community

Main Idea

The gospel of Jesus Christ creates community in a local church that is evidently supernatural in both its breadth (diversity) and its depth (commitment). But we get impatient, seeking to build community that "works" regardless of whether or not the gospel is believed and lived out. Our challenge as churches is to rely on the power of God to foster a community that showcases the power of the gospel.

Passage for study: John 13:31–35

Questions for Reflection and Discussion

1. How would you define church community? (The definition for the purposes of *The Compelling Community* is near the bottom of p. 13, but other definitions can also be helpful.)

2. What is the significance of the phrase "one another" in John 13:35?

3. In John 13, Jesus states that it is their love for one another that will mark out his disciples. Of all the virtues, why does *love* serve as the definitive sign of genuine discipleship? What aspects of the love between Christians can be seen only in the context of the local church?

4. Pages 22–24 contrast "gospel-revealing community" with "gospel-plus community." Gospel-revealing community consists of relationships that exist only because of the truth and power of the gospel. Gospel-plus community is community built on the gospel *plus* something else. Gospel-plus community *is not wrong or bad in itself*, but it doesn't necessarily show off the power of the gospel.

   a. What are some examples of gospel-revealing community in your church?

   b. What are some examples of gospel-plus community in your church?

5. Why is it important that at least some significant elements of a church's community be gospel-revealing (i.e., evidently supernatural)?

6. What pressures do churches face that encourage them to build community based on natural bonds that even non-Christians share (i.e., gospel-plus community)?

7. Look up Ephesians 2:11–22. Where do you see supernatural *breadth* of community? Where do you see supernatural *depth* of community?

8. Why was it important that the church in Ephesus be both Jew and Gentile from the very beginning? What would have happened if, instead, Paul had planted one church for Jewish Christians and another for Gentile Christians? What are some similarities and differences between the Jew-Gentile divide and modern parallels?

Matters for Prayer

- Pray that your congregation's belief in the good news of Jesus would be evidenced by the relationships members have with each other.
- Pray that you would increasingly want to spend your life for the glory of God.
- Pray that your church leaders would have wisdom to know how to shepherd your church toward "gospel-revealing" community.

Further reading: *The Beautiful Community: Diversity, Unity, and the Church at Its Best* by Irwyn Ince Jr. (IVP, 2020).

A Community Given by God

Main Idea

Gospel-revealing community is entirely dependent on the supernatural power of the gospel. Building it on the gospel and something else may grow our numbers, but it will compromise both our evangelism and our ability to follow Jesus Christ. As we think about church community, we must dig deep into the supernatural love that flows from our supernatural forgiveness by God in Christ.

Passage for study: Luke 7:36–50

Questions for Reflection and Discussion

1. In Luke 7:36–50, what is the point of Jesus's parable? What explains the difference between how Simon treated Jesus and how the woman treated Jesus?

2. In Luke 7:36–50, Jesus teaches us that our love for him flows out of our forgiveness by him. What must we do if we want our lives to be characterized by supernatural love?

3. Consider the illustration of God's glory leaving the temple (pp. 35–36). What are some of the more obviously supernatural elements of community in your church?

4. The bottom of page 36 asks, "Have you turned community-building into so much of a science that the supernatural has become optional?" Why is that practice harmful and dangerous? Why would it be a temptation for church leaders? How can you help them resist that temptation?

5. Can you think of an example of how someone came to Christ at least in part because of the witness of church community?

6. How does gospel-revealing community protect the doctrine of the church (pp. 39–42)? At a practical level, what does this look like?

7. What should you do when relating to others in your church requires more and deeper love than you can muster up on your own? In other words, how can you put 1 John 4:19 into practice?

Perhaps the most important aspects of this chapter are the last two points, found in the conclusion (pp.46–48). This last question relates to those points.

8. What is the danger of pursuing gospel-revealing community if many in a church don't yet believe the gospel?

Matters for Prayer

- Pray that you would grow in understanding the depth of Christ's love for you.
- Pray that those in your church who are not Christians would become Christians.
- Pray that the love the people in your congregation have for one another would be evidently supernatural and beyond what they could do in their own strength.

Further reading: *Conversion: How God Creates a People* by Michael Lawrence (Crossway, 2017).

3

Community Runs Deep

Main Idea

Our natural posture toward commitment is to commit once we're comfortable, to "try before you buy." But commitment to a church is different. That's because, as a basic part of what it means to follow Christ, God has called each of us to commit to a Christian congregation in ways that are significant and often uncomfortable. This outworking of Scripture's "one another" commands is an essential foundation for supernatural community—for the simple fact that relationship thrives with commitment. This is church membership made meaningful.

Passage for study: 1 John 4:19–21

Questions for Reflection and Discussion
1. According to 1 John 4:19–21, why is love for brothers and sisters in Christ critical for those who claim to love God?

2. What are some implications of this passage for your church? What are some implications for you?

3. Share an example of a time when someone in your church cared for you in a way that demonstrated a commitment that was deeper than what he or she probably would have expected to receive from the relationship. (In other words, provide an example of the "calling-based commitment" described on p. 54.) Alternatively, you could share an example of when *you* have cared for someone in this way, giving thanks to God.

4. Pick one verse per person in your group that describes the commitment a Christian is to make to other believers in Christ (some are listed on pp. 56–57). For each verse, try to articulate an aspect of that commitment that is different from other commitments people make in life. Which of the verses mentioned by your group can be applied *only* in the context of a local church?

5. Which of the "one another" commands on pages 56–57 do you think your congregation does especially well? Where does your congregation need to grow? How should understanding the concept of "calling-based commitment" help you as an individual Christian to grow?

6. What is your own answer to Kaitlin's objection to church membership: "Why do I need to sign a piece of paper to love people in my church?" (p. 53).

7. Read again the analogy of the warm-weather plants inside the United States Botanic Garden (p. 65). What are some ways in which the culture of commitment in your church accelerates the growth of relationships? How can you help this happen more?

8. What is one way in which the biblical principles in this chapter would prompt you to change how you relate to your church? Your answer could be something new to pray for, a different mindset for your friendships, different goals for fellowship, and so on.

Matters for Prayer
- Pray that your church would increasingly love one another, encourage one another, guard one another, and so forth.
- Pray that as your congregation deepens its commitment to each other, it would see deep friendships flourish.
- Pray that you would find real joy from your friendships at church.

Further reading: *Rediscover Church: Why the Body of Christ Is Essential* by Collin Hansen and Jonathan Leeman (Crossway, 2021).

4

Community Goes Broad

Main Idea

By the power of God's supernatural grace, a gospel-preaching church will ordinarily draw Christians from a wide variety of backgrounds, opinions, and personalities because they love Christ more than the comfort of similarity. As was the case in the Ephesian church, unity across surprising boundaries is an important way a church demonstrates the truth and power of the gospel. Very often, however, churches stifle such gospel-powered diversity by building community through ministry by similarity.

Passage for study: Ephesians 2:11–3:21

Questions for Reflection and Discussion

1. Trace for yourself Paul's argument from Ephesians 2:11 through 3:21 and outline it in your own words. If you're discussing this book in a group, you might do this together.

2. Why is unity between Jew and Gentile in Ephesians 2:11–3:21 a necessary implication of salvation by grace alone (2:1–10)? What does this have to do with the "manifold wisdom of God" being made known to the "rulers and authorities in the heavenly places" (3:10)?

3. How does Bill's story (p. 69) illustrate Ephesians 3:10 at work? In particular, what aspects of love in the church influenced him? (By the way, Bill retired soon after he was saved, was baptized, and joined my church. Today he is one of the best examples I can point to of someone who lives out the principles of this chapter.)

4. What differences in your congregation threaten unity (akin to the Jew/Gentile divide in Eph. 2)? Think of ethnic differences, cultural differences, class and tribal differences, and personality differences. Consider differences in gifting or ability, gender and marital status, politics and conviction, and so on. Which of these differences, if overrun by the gospel, would be most surprising to your non-Christian neighbors? For you personally, which are most and least present in your own friendships?

5. Page 79 explains that ministry by similarity isn't necessarily bad. It will likely be present to some extent in every church. But it is dangerous because the community it builds can appear to thrive even if the gospel is not believed or lived out. List some examples of ministry by similarity in your church. How has this

chapter adjusted your expectations and/or ambitions for those ministries?

6. Provide examples of how gospel-generated diversity is costly to the people in your church (pp. 80–81). How has it been costly to you?

7. Identify examples of "majority culture" and "minority culture" in your church (you may need to think beyond ethnicity). How can each culture do a better job of loving with brotherly affection (Rom. 12:10), of outdoing one another in showing honor (Rom. 12:10), and of welcoming each other (Rom. 15:7)?

8. What is one way in which the biblical principles in this chapter would prompt you to change how you relate to your church?

Matters for Prayer
- Pray that you would grow in the skill of building friendships with those you share little in common with other than Christ.
- Pray that non-Christians like Bill would be able to see the work the gospel has done in your church as it unites those who, apart from Christ, are very different.
- Pray that the leaders of your church would wisely encourage ministry by similarity when it is useful, and have the discernment to know when such ministry is counterproductive.

Further reading: *Talking about Race: Gospel Hope for Hard Conversations* by Isaac Adams (Zondervan, 2022).

PART 2

FOSTERING COMMUNITY

5

Preach to Equip Your Community

Main Idea

If gospel-revealing community is entirely dependent on faith, and if faith normally comes by hearing God's word (Rom. 10:17), then church community is ultimately powered by Scripture. But word-fueled community requires more than a sermon each week. It requires sermons that equip the congregation to apply God's word to each other. This chapter was written mainly with the preacher in mind, but the questions below are written mainly with congregants in mind.

Passage for study: Romans 10:14–17

Questions for Reflection and Discussion

1. Romans 10:14–17 describes the relationship between faith and hearing. What are some implications of this relationship for your life as a Christian and for your church? What does this tell you about the main purpose of the sermon you hear each week?

2. Page 89 says, "The challenge of building a culture of discipling is a challenge of faith." Why is that? What is a "culture of discipling"? Are you discipling anyone right now?

3. In Luke 12:48, Jesus tells us that "everyone to whom much was given, of him much will be required." What responsibility do you bear because of the biblical preaching you have received from your church (see pp. 96–97)?

4. How can you help others in your church benefit from the sermons that you hear together each week?

Matters for Prayer
- Pray that you would become a better hearer of God's preached word.
- Pray that faith-generating, God-honoring conversations about the weekly sermon and God's word would increasingly characterize your church.

Further reading: *Word-Centered Church: How Scripture Brings Life and Growth to God's People* by Jonathan Leeman (Moody, 2017).

6

Pray Together as a Community

Main Idea

A desire for God to build evidently supernatural community in our churches begins by asking him to do that work. This should happen as the church goes before God in prayer together, as a congregation. It should also happen as we each pray for our churches privately. This chapter was written primarily for the person who structures your church's weekly services, but the questions below are written with congregants in mind.

Passage for study: Daniel 9:1–23

Questions for Reflection and Discussion

1. What is the difference between private prayer and corporate prayer? Why is it important for a church to pray together, as a body?

2. In Daniel chapter 9, Daniel roots his request in God's reputation (Dan. 9:19). In other words, Daniel is asking God to answer because of God's overriding desire to be seen and known as good and glorious. With that goal in mind, what kind of concerns should dominate your prayer time when you pray together as a congregation?

3. How can you help corporate prayer feel more corporate, both when you're the one leading and when you're being led in prayer by someone else?

4. When you're praying privately for your church, what requests do you normally make? Will this chapter add or subtract from that list?

Matters for Prayer

- Pray that you and your congregation would regularly pray for your church.
- Pray that as God answers these prayers, he would be seen by those inside and outside your church as good, gracious, and glorious.

Further reading: *Prayer: How Praying Together Shapes the Church* by John Onwucheckwa (Crossway, 2018).

7

Build a Culture of
Spiritually Intentional Relationships

Main Idea
Church activity that is most fruitful is nearly always relational. This chapter suggests three strategies for deepening the relational fabric of a congregation: encouraging discipling and hospitality; encouraging people to center their lives on the local church; and emphasizing the privileges of church membership.

(If you're studying chaps. 7 and 8 together as suggested in the introduction, plan to spend most of your time on chap. 7.)

Passage for study: Colossians 1:28–29

Questions for Reflection and Discussion
1. According to Colossians 1:28–29, what were the apostle Paul's ministry goals? What aspects of Paul's example can you apply to your relationships at church?

2. Notice the repeated use of the word *we* in Colossians 1:28. Even Paul saw this maturing of believers as a group project. How has your own maturing in Christ been a group project for your church?

3. Name examples of people in your church who invest well in discipling and hospitality. What can you learn from them? What barriers exist that discourage others in your church from similar ministry?

4. Page 123 claims that "a life centered on the community of the local church is significantly more likely to be lived strategically in God's sight than a life where the local church languishes as a peripheral detail." To what extent do you agree with that statement? Why? What competitors for the hearts and time of the people in your congregation most distract them from a church-centric life? How about for you?

5. Pages 129–30 encourage a church to "restrict membership to regular attenders" and to "restrict involvement to members." Do you agree? Which of these two would be more challenging for your church? Why might these goals be important?*

---

* Aside from proclaiming the gospel and praying for God to give new birth, I think that these two objectives are perhaps the most important things a church can do to lay the foundation for the kind of vision described in chapters 1–4. Meaningful membership articulates the kind of love Christians are to live out in the church, but for many churches, membership isn't much of a commitment.

_____

_____

_____

_____

Matters for Prayer

- Pray that you and the other members of your church would more fully live out the idea that an essential aspect of following Jesus is helping others follow Jesus.
- Pray that God would give your congregation creativity and grace to overcome obstacles it might face to discipling and hospitality.

Further reading: *The Trellis and the Vine: The Ministry Mind-Shift That Changes Everything*, 2nd ed., by Colin Marshall and Tony Payne (Matthias Media, 2021).

8

Structural Obstacles to Biblical Community

Main Idea

Resistance to biblical community is hardwired into the infrastructure of many of our churches. In particular, despite our best intentions, the design of church staff, the church schedule, church music, church services, and church ministries can complicate our efforts to encourage deep, relational ministry across boundaries within the church. These elements of church life can accomplish great good, but we should assess them in light of their impact on biblical community.

(You might skip this chapter if you're studying chaps. 7 and 8 together.)

Passage for study: 1 Corinthians 3:5–15

Questions for Reflection and Discussion

1. As you read through the potential obstacles to biblical community in this chapter, which was most surprising or thought-provoking?

2. Did the sections about church staff and church ministries encourage you in any way to recalibrate your expectations for your church's staff and ministries (pp. 134–38, 146–49)?

3. Page 149 warns against equating church community with small groups. For which aspects of church community are small groups well designed? Where do small groups fall short of capturing the kind of community that this book has been discussing?

Matters for Prayer
- Pray that God would bless the efforts of your church staff to equip the members of your congregation to minister to each other.
- Pray that your church leaders would have wisdom as they consider how to structure the infrastructure and operations of your church so that they serve the unity of the congregation.

Further reading: *How to Build a Healthy Church: A Practical Guide for Deliberate Leadership*, 2nd ed., by Mark Dever and Paul Alexander (Crossway, 2021).

PART 3

PROTECTING COMMUNITY

9

Addressing Discontentment in the Church

Main Idea

In a fallen world, discontentment with your church will be inevitable, and it will threaten unity. The first-century church offers a model for how to work through threats to unity, with the congregation taking initiative to protect that unity. When church members speak about discontentment or disagreement with the church, it's important to note whether these disagreements are over gospel issues (which are more important than unity) or secondary issues (in which case gospel unity is paramount).

Passage for study: Acts 6:1–7

Questions for Reflection and Discussion

1. How would you describe the apostles' priorities in Acts 6? What can we learn from them?

2. What are some of the most important lessons your congregation could learn from how the Acts 6 congregation addressed disagreement and discontentment?

3. The bottom of page 156 states that "ultimately, it is the congregation's job to protect unity." What can church members do to protect unity in the church?

4. Consider the following five problems that your church might face. Assign each to one of the four boxes in the grid on page 166 and indicate what role you as a member of the congregation should play in addressing it.

- Church leadership proposes a budget that you think is too aggressive.

- A deacon in your church is known to be having an adulterous affair, and the church allows him to continue serving as a deacon.

- Your pastor routinely posts political commentary on social media that, in your opinion, is dividing the church.

- Given that a majority of families in your church homeschool their children and some are quite vocal about the benefits of that option, you feel the church can be a difficult place for those who send their kids to public school. You suggest your pastor speak up about this. He tells you that he does not want to wade into that debate because it would further inflame this threat to church unity.

- You and the other members of your small group agree that the pastor's new car is too flashy and expensive.

Matters for Prayer
- Pray that God would help you to love the unity of your church more than your own comfort.
- Pray that God would allow you to see threats to unity in your church and give you the wisdom to know how to help.

Further reading: *Conscience: What It Is, How to Train It, and Loving Those Who Differ* by Andy Naselli and J. D. Crowley (Crossway, 2016).

10

Addressing Sin in the Church

Main Idea

A church should be a place where conversations are full of grace yet honest about sin and struggle. Careful adherence to Jesus's instructions in Matthew 18 (about how to address sin privately and when to bring that conversation to the whole church) will help shift a church's culture in this direction.

Passage for study: Matthew 18:15–17

Questions for Reflection and Discussion

1. Which of the two hypothetical churches on pages 169–70 comes closest to describing what your church would be if all the members had the same instincts and convictions that you do ("all law, no grace" or "all grace, no law")? Hopefully neither is a particularly accurate description.

2. What is needed for a church to have a culture "where it is normal for people to have deep and honest conversations about their spiritual lives . . . *and* where the gospel of grace is an everyday answer to struggle with sin" (p. 171)?

3. Which of Christ's commands in Matthew 18:15–17 do you find most challenging to obey? Why?

4. Which aspects of Jesus's teaching in Matthew 18:15–17 help a church to build a culture of grace in the church? Which aspects help a church to build a culture of honesty about sin and struggle?

_____

_____

_____

_____

_____

Matters for Prayer

- Pray that conversations between church members would be honest and transparent about sin and struggle and, at the same time, characterized by grace and charity.
- Pray for wisdom so that the next time you find a brother or sister caught in sin, you will be able to love them well. Pray for humility so that you can be helped by others when you're caught in sin.

Further reading: *The Rule of Love: How the Local Church Should Reflect God's Love and Authority* by Jonathan Leeman (Crossway, 2018).

PART 4

────────

COMMUNITY AT WORK

11

Evangelize as a Community

Main Idea

Though evangelism is normally personal (it begins with a Christian telling someone the gospel), it is ideally also corporate because the community of the local church is profound evidence for the truth of the Christian gospel. As church members, we should talk about life in a congregation with our non-Christian friends, seek to mix our Christian and non-Christian circles of friendship, and take initiative to engage fellow church members in opportunities for service and evangelism outside the church.

Passage for study: Deuteronomy 4:5–8

Questions for Reflection and Discussion

1. According to Deuteronomy 4:5–8, what effect was the nation of Israel to have on the nations around them as they obeyed God's commands? What parallels do you see with God's calling for churches today?

2. Page 190 asks the question "In [a postindustrial, postrural, post-Christian] world, how do we display the corporate witness of the church to a watching world?" What are your answers to that question? Feel free to name strategies from pages 190–93 and to add to that list.

3. As a group, think of one good way to introduce non-Christian family, friends, or coworkers to the community of your church. Then put it into practice.

Matters for Prayer

- Pray that your congregation would be active in sharing the good news about Jesus with non-Christian friends, coworkers, and family.
- Pray that some of these unbelievers would see evidence of Jesus's love as they observe how the people in your congregation love one another.

Further reading: *Evangelism: How the Whole Church Speaks of Jesus* by Mack Stiles (Crossway, 2014).

·

12

Fracture Your Community
(for the Community of Heaven)

Main Idea

Sometimes a new church can be started or an old one restarted by "hiving off" a section of an existing congregation. This has the obvious advantage of seeding the new church with the healthy community DNA of the original church. But the strain on the original church is more than merely sending out one or two people, and it forces churches to ask the question, "Is our DNA worth replicating yet?"

Passage for study: Psalm 67

Questions for Reflection and Discussion

If your church is in the process of sending out a group of members to plant a new church or to restart an old one, you might skip the discussion questions below and talk through the questions on pages 206–7 instead.

1. In Psalm 67:1 the psalmist quotes the priestly blessing of Aaron from Numbers 6:24–26, and in verse 2 he supplies a purpose for that blessing. What is that purpose?

2. Psalm 67 was written to the Old Testament people of God; how would the purpose statement of verse 2 apply to the New Testament people of God (the church)?

3. What are the advantages and disadvantages of the "yogurt" model of church planting (p. 199), where a sizable portion of the congregation goes off to start the new church?

4. As you read through the list of questions on pages 201 and 202 ("Is Your Church Community Ready to Replicate"), where can you praise God for questions you answer yes to? Where do you need to pray that God would do further work in your congregation?

Matters for Prayer
- Pray that your church would have the privilege of helping to start new churches.
- Pray for your church leaders to have discernment as they determine how to best lead your church toward church planting endeavors.

Further reading: *Planting by Pastoring: A Vision for Starting a Healthy Church* by Nathan Knight (Crossway, 2023)

Conclusion

Main Idea

Gospel community (what we see) is the natural partner to gospel proclamation (what we hear), and we need both for churches to continue in gospel health and gospel witness.

Questions for Reflection and Discussion

1. The top of page 210 points to underappreciation of the importance of gospel community as a common source of failure in churches that are too entertainment-oriented and also in churches that are too legalistic. Do you agree? Why or why not?

2. Read through the sentence-level summaries of each chapter on pages 210–11. Which of these topics do you most need to think more about?

_____

_____

_____

_____

_____

.

Next Steps

Every book you read is a stewardship from God, and *The Compelling Community* is no exception. Assuming you found at least one useful takeaway in this book or in the discussions you had about the book, you should determine how you will put that knowledge to work for Jesus. Below, list what you would like to do in response to what you learned. These might include:

- A conversation you will have with someone in your church.
- Things you might start teaching.
- Things you need to stop doing.
- Ways you will think differently about your church.
- A passage of Scripture you would like to study further.
- A book you will read.
- Priorities for regular prayer.

1. _____

2. _____

3. _____

_____

4. _____

_____

IX **9Marks**

Building Healthy Churches

9Marks exists to equip church leaders with a biblical vision and practical resources for displaying God's glory to the nations through healthy churches.

To that end, we want to see churches characterized by these nine marks of health:

1. Expositional Preaching
2. Gospel Doctrine
3. A Biblical Understanding of Conversion and Evangelism
4. Biblical Church Membership
5. Biblical Church Discipline
6. A Biblical Concern for Discipleship and Growth
7. Biblical Church Leadership
8. A Biblical Understanding of the Practice of Prayer
9. A Biblical Understanding and Practice of Missions

Find all our Crossway titles and other resources at 9Marks.org.

IX 9Marks

THE COMPELLING COMMUNITY

*Where God's Power Makes
a Church Attractive*

**MARK DEVER &
JAMIE DUNLOP**

In *The Compelling Community*, authors Mark Dever and
Jamie Dunlop help pastors create authentic fellowship
within their church communities. Ideally used alongside the
study guide, this book teaches commitment and diversity
through theological principles and practical advice.

For more information, visit **crossway.org**.